CONFIDENT YOU

AN INTROVERT'S GUIDE TO SUCCESS IN LIFE AND BUSINESS

D1359554

WRITTEN BY:

REBECCA LIVERMORE

www.ProfessionalContentCreation.com

S.J. SCOTT

www.HabitBooks.com

Disclaimer

No part of this publication may be reproduced or transmitted in any form or by any means, mechanical or electronic, including photocopying or recording, or by any information storage and retrieval system, or transmitted by email without permission in writing from the publisher.

While all attempts have been made to verify the information provided in this publication, neither the author nor the publisher assumes any responsibility for errors, omissions or contrary interpretations of the subject matter herein.

This book is for entertainment purposes only. The views expressed are those of the author alone, and should not be taken as expert instruction or commands. The reader is responsible for his or her own actions.

Adherence to all applicable laws and regulations, including international, federal, state and local laws governing professional licensing, business practices, advertising and all other aspects of doing business in the US, Canada or any other jurisdiction is the sole responsibility of the purchaser or reader.

Neither the author nor the publisher assumes any responsibility or liability whatsoever on the behalf of the purchaser or reader of these materials.

Any perceived slight of any individual or organization is purely unintentional.

Table of Contents

As a way of saying *thanks* for your purchase, I'm offering a free report that's exclusive to my book and blog readers.

In *77 Good Habits to Live a Better Life*, you'll discover a variety of routines that can help you in many different areas of your life. You will learn how to make lasting changes to your work, success, learning, health and sleep habits.

Go here to grab *77 Good Habits to Live a Better Life*:
http://www.developgoodhabits.com/free

Your Free Gift (2)

Are you an introvert who would love to make a living from the comfort of your own home? If so, you're in luck; due to all of the opportunities online, the time has never been better!

An Introvert's Guide to Starting an Online Business provides a simple step-by-step plan for making a living doing something you love, in a way that fits with your unique personality and gifts.

Go here to grab your free copy of *An Introvert's Guide to Starting an Online:*
http://professionalcontentcreation.com/introvert-business-guide-book

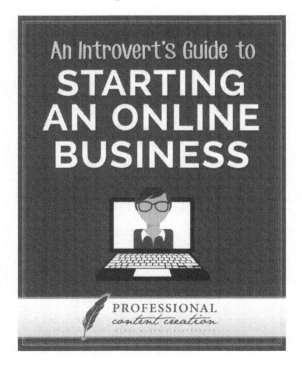

The Challenge of Introversion

B eing an introvert can be frustrating.

In a world where extroversion is applauded, it's easy to feel left out in the cold. If you're an introvert, you no doubt have experienced this challenge. You know it's important to be outgoing, social and a good leader, yet these behaviors don't seem natural.

The truth is that success in life often comes down to how well you sell yourself. This means behaving in a manner that doesn't seem congruent with what's inside. In simple terms, the world around us requires introverts to behave in an extroverted manner.

On the other hand, it's dangerous to think you need to become an extrovert to be successful.

First, it's almost impossible to change your core personality. Sure, you can learn how to *behave* differently in certain situations, but you won't change what's on the inside.

Second, there are many positives to being an introvert. Introverts are often analytical, forward-thinking and sensitive to the feelings of others. In fact, as you'll see throughout this book, many of the significant changes in human history are due to the actions of introverts.

Yes, we live in a world that often rewards extroverted behavior. But we also live in a world filled with the accomplishments of introverts. The trick here is to learn how to merge the positive habits of extroverts with the introspective habits you possess.

All of this will be covered in the following book, *Confident You: An Introvert's Guide to Success in Life and Business.*

About Confident You

This book started with a message to Steve's email list. The message asked subscribers to describe the number one challenge they face as introverts.

The response was overwhelming...

Steve received more than 300 emails, with many of the responses exceeding 500 words. In fact, the total word count of these comments is greater than the word count of this book.

Needless to say, many people have strong feelings when it comes to the topic of introversion. Instead of writing this book from just *our* perspectives, we decided to include many of the words we received from readers just like you. You will hear about their specific challenges, develop an understanding of what they go through every day, and perhaps learn how to overcome the challenges you currently face.

You will also discover how being an introvert can be a good thing. In fact, we feel you have a lot to offer to the world. Without introverts, society would be full of outgoing and social people but a lot fewer artists, analysts, scientists, doctors, writers, engineers, and designers.

We're not out to "fix" you.

We want to make that one point abundantly clear. When it comes to the topic of introversion, many books and websites push the notion that, *"If you're an introvert, there's something wrong with you, and our goal is to fix you!"*

Let us state from the outset that we're not out to "fix" introverts.

Steve and Rebecca are both introverts, and we understand first-hand that being an introvert isn't wrong, it's just the way you are. Introversion is something that is hardwired into some people, so it's an unchangeable part of your social makeup.

Unfortunately, the world often celebrates and rewards extroverts. Because of this tendency, extroverts may find it easier to succeed in various aspects of life, leaving introverts out in the cold.

Instead of trying to make you an extrovert, the goal of this book is to help you capitalize on all the positive aspects of being an introvert. At the same time, this book will also help you learn ways to compensate and, when appropriate, overcome some of the less positive aspects of introversion.

What you'll discover in *Confident You* is a series of strategies to help you become more extroverted in business and social situations. These strategies will help you get ahead without being fake or compromising who you are on the inside.

About Us

Obviously, Steve (or "S.J.") is an introvert. He runs the blog Develop Good Habits, and he's the author of a series of habit-related titles, all of which can be found at HabitBooks.com. The goal of his content is to show how continuous habit development can lead to a better life.

Steve considers himself to be an introspective person who doesn't enjoy being in the spotlight. Yet, as his business has grown over the past few years, he has had to become more extroverted in order grow with it. This includes doing podcast interviews, giving presentations and attending in-person conferences.

While Steve doesn't always enjoy these activities, he's also taught himself a few "tricks" to find that sweet spot between being an introvert and being an extrovert (when the situation calls for it).

Rebecca is also an introvert. In her younger years, she battled extreme shyness to the point that some people have made comments such as, *"You were so quiet, I didn't even realize you were there."* Ouch! As such, she understands how painful introversion and shyness can be, and what it's like to have her very presence—not to mention her contributions—go unnoticed.

At the same time, the positive aspects of introversion have actually helped her achieve a lot of success in both her personal and professional life. She's the owner of <u>Professional Content Creation</u>, and a freelance writer and content strategy consultant for small businesses. She's married and the mom of two young adults.

While she enjoys solitude and quiet, she's learned how to "act" extroverted in limited situations. This balance has helped her capitalize on the benefits of introversion while overcoming some of the negative aspects of it.

How This Book is Structured

First off, you have probably noticed that we use the third-person tense (e.g., "Steve remembers…" or "Rebecca suggests…") when sharing anecdotes about our experiences. This was done specifically to make it easier for you to follow the narrative of the book. We admit it's a bit clunky, but you'll find it's easier to grasp the information if you know who is telling the story.

Next, you'll notice that the narrative of this book includes many anecdotes from readers like you. This was done intentionally because we wanted to show that some aspects of introversion are a common challenge for *many* people. Perhaps it'll give you a sense of comfort to know that many people out there are going through the same thing.

Finally, the format of this book is pretty straightforward. We'll start with an overview of introversion. Then we'll ask you to take a quick test to identify your core personality trait. And then the "meat" of this book will cover the 15 specific challenges introverts face, with quick solutions for overcoming them.

But, before we dive into the content, we want to thank everyone who took the time to leave a response to our survey. Words can't express how grateful we are to those who were brave enough to describe their experiences. The book would be nothing without your help, so we dedicate the following to you.

Okay, we have a lot of ground to cover in a short amount of time, so let's kick things off with a simple definition of what it means to be an introvert.

What is an Introvert?

Many people confuse introversion with shyness. While many introverts are also shy, the primary characteristic of introverts is that their internal "battery" drains when spending time with others, and they "recharge" by being alone.

To elaborate on this idea, here are some common characteristics we've observed, experienced ourselves or heard from our readers. Introverts:

- Are often driven by emotions, concepts, feelings and impressions.
- Tend to prefer to think before acting.
- Can be sensitive to sensory inputs and are sometimes overwhelmed by excess stimuli.
- Often get overwhelmed by the external world and often feel uncomfortable in large groups.
- Have a developed sense of self and are self-reflective.
- Dislike small talk, often feeling like it's fake, phony, and meaningless.
- Can be fiercely independent, usually preferring their own company over others'.
- Cause minimal drama and work well with others.
- Are perceptive and see connections that others may miss.
- Can be good listeners.

- Are often better writers than speakers, since writing allows them time to compose their thoughts.
- Are passionate about areas that interest them.
- Can be very comfortable and social in one-on-one situations.
- May not speak unless they have something of value to contribute.

Obviously, there is a danger when speaking in generalities. As you'll learn, we all come in many shapes, sizes and personalities. This means you can't look at these traits and assume they describe every introvert.

The truth is some prefer the company of others over isolation and some even prefer regularly engaging in small talk. The important point here is to understand how *your* introversion works and to learn how to overcome the specific challenges you personally face.

Also, contrary to popular opinion, some introverts are very social. In fact, some of the people you view as being extroverts are actually introverts. In reality, it's not about what you see on the outside but how you feel on the inside.

Which is More Commons: Introversion or Extroversion?

It's difficult to know the exact percentage of people in the world who are introverts. According to an article in Psychology Today, between 16 and 50 percent of the population are introverts, while 50 to 74 percent of the population are extroverts.

On the other hand, Susan Cain, author of *Quiet: The Power of Introverts in a World That Can't Stop Talking* states that at least one-third of the population are introverts.

While precise percentages are hard to come by, one thing is certain: there are a lot of introverts in the world. However, introverts are a minority, and as such, they are often viewed as different, and perhaps a bit odd.

This difference has, at times, resulted in a misunderstanding of introverts. From a young age, many introverts are even told to act more extroverted. If you're an introvert, such "encouragement" from well-meaning friends, family members, teachers and bosses may have left you feeling defective, but nothing could be further from the truth.

Never Forget This…

There is nothing wrong with being an introvert.

Let us say that again.

There is nothing wrong with being an introvert!

In the same way that being left-handed or right-handed is neither good nor bad, but rather just a part of your genetic makeup, introversion is neither good nor bad. It's just who you are.

You don't have to become an extrovert to achieve great things. That's good news because you can't stop being an introvert. Trying to fight who you are will only lead to lifelong unhappiness. That said, there *are* some challenges when it comes to being an introvert. So not only will we cover the positive aspects, we'll also show you how to get ahead in a world of extroverts <u>without</u> compromising who you are.

Introverts Don't Have to Be the Life of the Party…

But *showing up* to the party is a good idea.

Steve and Rebecca met for the first time during a one-day, in-person business mastermind in San Diego.

Bert, an extroverted attendee, didn't want to wait until the day of the event to meet everyone in the group, so he organized a "meet and greet" dinner on the night before the mastermind.

In spite of their introverted tendencies, Steve and Rebecca (who hadn't yet met) chose to get together with the other attendees for dinner. They both recognized that, while the training they would receive at the business breakthrough was important, the <u>real value</u> would come from people they'd meet at the event.

You see, Bert demonstrated the classic behavior of an extroverted "connector," while Steve and Rebecca simply showed up to the event.

The point here? As an introvert, you don't have to be the life of the party to be successful, but it does help to show up to the party if you want to "eat the cake."

Lessons from Famous Introverts

While introverts may appear to be at a disadvantage when it comes to success (at least in the way that society defines it), there are many introverts who have helped shape the world. Some names might seem obvious, but others will probably surprise you.

Here are a few examples of famous introverts and their primary accomplishment(s):

- Warren Buffett, one of the wealthiest people in the world, and a great philanthropist
- J.K. Rowling, an extremely successful author
- Albert Einstein, physicist and Nobel Prize winner
- Mahatma Gandhi, known for non-violent resistance
- Larry Page, Google co-founder
- Steve Wozniak, Apple co-founder
- Bill Gates, Microsoft founder and philanthropist
- Angelina Jolie, an actress who, by her own admission, has very few friends
- Lady Gaga, a pop star who is shy and often feels like she doesn't fit in
- Christina Aguilera, a pop star who, by her own admission, has always been an introvert and feels like an outsider because of it

- Eleanor Roosevelt, former first lady, who has been quoted as saying, *"Friendship with oneself is all important, because without it one cannot be friends with anyone else in the world."*
- Laura Bush, former first lady, is a prime example of someone who is an introvert, but not shy, as demonstrated by her public speaking skills, sense of humor, and ability to handle the press with grace and dignity.
- Rosa Parks, civil-rights icon, who was naturally shy but courageous when it mattered most.
- Roy Rogers, singer and actor, who admits that, even though he loved show business, being an introvert didn't make it easy to make a living in this industry.

(**Side note**: If you want to learn more about these famous introverts, be sure to check out this article on Urban Times: http://bit.ly/1NWL39v and this one on Huffington Post: http://huff.to/1Aj4iWe.)

Did any of these names surprise you?

The reason we included them here is to show that many introverts can be shy, even if they are widely considered to be the epitome of outgoing extroverted personalities. As we've already said, the main difference between introverts and extroverts is how often they need time alone to recharge their batteries.

We also hope to show that introverts can and do succeed at just about any job or career imaginable. Their best contributions often happen when they team up with extroverts.

For example, Steve Jobs and Steve Wozniak partnered together when launching Apple Computers. Odds are, they couldn't have succeeded on their own. It took the combined forces of Wozniak's revolutionary computer and Jobs' natural ability to sell.

Jobs was the extrovert who made the deals and served as the public face of Apple, but without Wozniak doing the work on Apple I and Apple II, very little would have been accomplished.

Are You an Introvert?

Ideas of introversion and extroversion were first popularized by psychologist Carl Jung in the early 1920s. Since then, there have been many studies performed and articles written on the difference between the two types of personalities.

Not every psychology theory views introverts exactly the same way, but they all agree that introversion is a distinct personality type.

These ideas are currently used (in some form) in every single psychology personality test.

Here are three of the most popular personality tests:

- Meyers-Briggs Type Indicator (MBTI)
- Cantrell's 16 Personality Factor Questionnaire
- Minnesota Multiphasic Personality Inventory (MMPI)

Although these tests are some of the most popular ways to assess personality, Rebecca and Steve both prefer this free personality test: www.16personalities.com/free-personality-test.

In fact, we recommend you spend 10 minutes taking the free personality test before continuing with the rest of the book.

What is Your "Flavor" of Introversion?

In 1945, the seeds of the famous ice-cream chain, Baskin Robbins, were planted. Over time, the company became known for offering 31 flavors of ice cream (one for each day of the month) at a single time. While the primary ingredients of ice cream are always the same (cream and sugar, for example), <u>each flavor is distinctly different</u>.

In the same way that not all ice cream is vanilla, not all introverts are the same flavor. There are nearly as many differences among introverts as there are between introverts and extroverts.

As we've mentioned previously, both Steve and Rebecca are introverts. However, as they've discovered while working on this book together, and as you'll soon discover, they aren't exactly the same "flavor."

In the same way that not all flavors of ice cream appeal to you, you may find that not every chapter in this book is "your flavor."

To make any useful decisions, it is important to have an idea of which style (or flavor) of introversion applies to your personality. This will allow you to cherry-pick the right advice and strategies for your particular situation. So let's talk about the differences among the eight types of introverted personalities.

8 Types of Introverts

One of the best tips for success is to understand both your strengths and weaknesses.

When Steve took the 16 personality test that we mentioned before, he discovered that his "flavor" is The Defender. When Rebecca took the test, she learned that she is The Logistician.

After taking the test, you probably learned a few things about yourself. If you're anything like Steve, then you may not have liked some of what you read.

Understanding your own qualities is an excellent starting point, but it's equally important to understand the characteristics of people you interact with on a regular basis. To learn more, we recommend taking a close look at the 16 different personality types listed here: www.16personalities.com/personality-types

Now, since the focus of this book is on introversion, we'll skip over the eight types of extroverts and cover the eight types of introverts.

#1. INTP: Introverted / Intuitive / Thinking / Perceiving – (4.8% of men, 1.8% of women)

"The Logician"

- Logical
- Creative
- Inventive
- Love ideas and theories
- Enthusiastic about their passions
- Rebels
- Reserved
- Hard to get to know
- Individualist
- Not leaders or followers

#2. INTJ: Introverted / Intuitive / Thinking / Judging – (3.3% of men, 0.8% of women)

"The Architect"

- Independent
- Good planners
- Find patterns
- Committed
- High standards
- Judgmental
- Good leaders
- Self-confident
- Hates restrictions

#3. INFP: Introverted / Intuitive / Feeling / Perceiving – (4.1% of men, 4.6% of women)

"The Mediator"

- Reflective
- Quiet
- Idealistic
- Follow personal values
- Loyal to people who know them
- Laid back/ flexible
- Calm
- Good communicator
- Enjoy helping others

#4. ISTJ: Introverted / Sensing / Thinking / Judging – (16.4% of men, 6.9% of women

"The Logistician"

- Quiet
- Serious
- Responsible
- Duty oriented
- Practical
- Logical
- Goal oriented
- No-nonsense
- Traditional
- Love order
- Love organization

#5. ISFJ: Introverted / Sensing / Feeling / Judging – (8.1% of men, 19.4% of women)

"The Defender"

- Kind
- Conscientious
- Stable
- Practical
- Responsible
- Puts needs of others over their own
- Good people skills
- Empathetic

#6. INFJ: Introverted / Intuitive / Feeling / Judging – (1.3% of men, 1.6% of women)

"The Advocate"

- Good insight into others
- Sensitive
- Firm values
- Strong opinions
- Decisive
- Strong willed
- Make connections with others

#7. ISFP: Introverted / Sensing / Feeling / Perceiving – (7.6% of men, 9.9% of women)

"The Adventurer"

- Live for the present
- Care for others
- Independent
- Sensitive
- Creative
- Artistic
- Enjoy new things/experiences/people
- Unpredictable

#8. ISTP: Introverted / Sensing / Thinking / Perceiving – (8.5% of men, 2.4% of women)

"The Virtuoso"

- Tolerant
- Reserved
- Flexible
- Quiet
- Good at the way things interact
- Good with mechanical items
- Analytical
- Optimistic
- Good in crisis
- Stubborn
- Easily bored

As you can see, introverts have both positive and negative characteristics. This means we each have our own unique challenges when it comes to our personal and professional lives.

For the remainder of this book, we'll go over 15 of these challenges and outline specific strategies you can use to overcome them. As we mentioned before, some won't apply to you, so feel free to skip past these sections.

Challenge #1: Perception of Rudeness or Aloofness

Most introverts are quiet by nature. Unfortunately, this often creates the perception that we're rude, aloof, or even stuck up. This couldn't be further from the truth. While all people (introverts and extroverts alike) have areas in which they need to grow, introversion in and of itself isn't an indication that someone is selfish.

Yes, there *are* selfish introverts, just like there are selfish extroverts, but this trait has nothing to do with whether someone is an introvert or extrovert.

In a poll comment, Paula D. brought up a problem most non-introverts would never understand. We feel that it illustrates one of the major divisions between introverts and extroverts. (In other words, most introverts will "get it," while most extroverts won't.)

Paula's favorite way to relax is to go to a restaurant alone and enjoy dinner while reading books on her iPhone. She often sits at the bar while doing this and is dismayed when she is approached by people who want to strike up a conversation. She doesn't want to be rude, but resents the imposition on her critical recharge time (and perhaps shows the body language of someone who wants to be left alone).

Her desire to be left alone isn't selfish any more than the extrovert's desire to talk to strangers. It's merely a difference between introverts and extroverts, with neither approach being right or wrong.

The Root of the Misunderstanding

A major problem with introversion revolves around living in a world where extroversion is praised and valued.

For example:

Extroverts are often seen as living in the ideal "happy" state. They may not actually be any happier than introverts, but since they're viewed as being outgoing, they are often perceived as being happier than introverts.

Since a high value is placed on being social, people tend to undervalue people who are quieter, which leads to the perception that introverts are indifferent or uncaring.

Solution to Challenge #1

Are you often perceived as rude or aloof? If so, here are a few ways to overcome this perception.

Strategy 1:

Turn your introversion into an advantage. Look for the ways it can benefit your personal or professional life. Perhaps there is an aspect of your job where it's important to have a quieter, introspective personality.

For instance, in a poll comment, John N. shared that being an introvert gives him an edge as an investigator in the stock market. It enables him to stay in the background as he analyzes what he observes.

Strategy 2:

Don't be so concerned about what others think of you. What you think of yourself is more important than the opinions of strangers.

As an example, Steve "gets" Paula's problem about wanting to enjoy a book during a solo dinner. It's something he doesn't do as often he'd like, so he really enjoys this time alone. This doesn't make him asocial. It's more about enjoying private time.

Now, expressing the desire to be left alone can be tricky. Although you want your "me" time, you shouldn't be rude to people if they're simply trying to start conversations.

One subtle trick is to let your body language speak for you. If you're engaged in an activity and someone insists on striking up a conversation, give short answers, and when they are done speaking, look back at your book as a way of giving off an "I want to read" vibe.

Ultimately, this all comes down to your personal values. If people just don't get it, you can choose to be a little rude and let the other person know you're enjoying a private moment. Sometimes the simplest solution is to be blunt.

Strategy 3:

Make more of an effort to be polite to the people you know. For instance, Rebecca always takes the time to express her care to the important people in her life. She feels this is more important to her than worrying about how she's perceived in a public setting.

With her friends and family, Rebecca goes out of her way to show interest in ways that are comfortable to her as an introvert. She sends cards, "likes" her friends' comments on Facebook, and reaches out occasionally via email to let friends know she's thinking of them.

Since Rebecca doesn't say much, perhaps she's viewed as a bit aloof in public settings. However, her efforts to express care for the people in her life demonstrate how much those people mean to her.

Strategy 4:

Practice general politeness. Even the most introverted people can say "please" and "thank you." Practicing old-fashioned manners is an easy way to indicate that you aren't a stuck-up snob.

Challenge #2: Exhaustion from Overstimulation

Exhaustion from overstimulation is a huge problem for many introverts. In fact, not only do Steve and Rebecca both struggle with this, but many respondents to our survey described how they felt emotionally drained after spending a lot of time in social situations.

As an introvert, it's important to understand what overstimulates you and do what you can to minimize those things.

For example, Rebecca is very sensitive to hearing others talk around her. Her husband loves listening to talk radio, which stresses her out, so she often asks him to use headphones so he can still enjoy the shows without it distracting her.

Bottom line: The key to overcoming this challenge is to be aware of what overstimulates you and then devise coping strategies.

Highly Sensitive Persons (HSPs)

As a side note, if you find yourself constantly overstimulated by your immediate environment, then you might be a highly sensitive person or HSP.

Neither Steve nor Rebecca are HSP, so we can only commiserate with the struggles of being an HSP introvert. That said, we did receive a few responses from people who have this personality trait. The difference between them is that, while introverts occasionally feel drained, HSPs often feel drained from almost all of the following:

- Loud sounds and noise
- Light
- Colors
- Social interactions
- Touch
- Small talk
- Sales calls
- Meetings
- Talking on the phone
- Networking
- Caffeine

If you know or suspect that you, a family member or friend are HSP, Elaine Aron wrote an excellent book that talks about this condition, explains why many introverts fall into this category and offers suggestions for interacting with the world.

You can also visit her website (http://hsperson.com) where she has a lot of helpful information as well as self-tests to help you determine if you or your child are HSP.

Now, whether you're an introvert or someone with HSP, overstimulation is a challenge that many of us deal with on a regular basis, so let's go over a few ways you can deal with this issue.

Solutions to Challenge #2

Introverts all have different activities that overstimulate them. For instance, Steve has no problem with caffeine, but others find that too much caffeine makes them feel out of sorts. He also enjoys working in crowded and noisy places such as Starbucks, while Rebecca works best in absolute silence and only writes in public places when it's absolutely necessary.

Finding a solution to overstimulation is all about understanding what exhausts you and knowing how to respond when you encounter your triggers.

Think of it this way: All introverts have a "battery" that might hold a lesser *or* greater charge than the "batteries" other people have. Different activities can drain this battery at different rates, so it's important to know what type of activity overstimulates you the most.

Furthermore, introverts can do anything extroverts can do. The difference is that an introvert can only do it for so long before burning out, while an extrovert often gets enjoyment and energy from the same level of social interaction. This means the best thing an introvert can do is to take breaks before and after participating in activities that drain them. Taking a break gives you time to recharge, which can often be enough to prevent exhaustion or burnout.

To be successful throughout your life, it's important to consider the charge of your "social battery" at all times.

Take private "me time" before social events and make sure your battery is fully charged so you can be at your best in these situations. It also helps to plan for alone time after social events so you can relax and unwind.

Enjoy your time alone, and don't feel guilty about it. Understand that this time is as important as the time you spend engaging with others.

What should you do with this time?

Here are a few suggestions:

- Take long, hot showers
- Watch movies
- Practice musical instruments
- Shop
- Read
- Write
- Sit on the couch with a beer and relax
- Play video games
- Spend time online (Social media is not really "social," so some introverts find it relaxing.)
- Travel
- Watch TV or Netflix
- Sit with pets and take time to relax
- Sit with others in companionable silence (like when you are watching TV together)

If you're looking for additional ways to relax, then check out this response from John E. He truly understands his introverted behavior and knows to how to use it to his benefit.

"I used to think that being introverted meant that there was something wrong with me. I could not connect with others nor maintain relationships. I was lonely and my confidence suffered because I did not have a large group of friends and felt that having groups of people was necessary in order to be successful.

I adapted by learning how to network, be personable, developing good communication skills and active listening. I became gregarious for career purposes.

However, as an introvert it is incredibly draining to be in social situations. I have found ways to keep my energy levels up by going to my car on lunch breaks, taking a 30-minute nap and reading books that cause introspection in order to get a quick recharge."

We love these strategies because John does a great job of explaining the negative feelings that some introverts feel, but he also shows how he's able to overcome them in social situations and recharge his "battery" afterward.

He also went on to describe the interpersonal relationship with his wife, who is an extrovert.

"I am also married. My wife did not understand why I did not want to go out on a Friday night. The amount of energy I would have to expend throughout the weekday being gregarious and social is exhausting. I need to recharge at nights and retreat inward for two hours. So we made a compromise that we would plan weekend activities in advance and not go out on Friday nights."

As his final tip for being a successful, "outgoing" introvert, John mentions how he works his life to accommodate both his introversion and professional need to be social.

"I also wake up at 5 AM every morning in order to have my 'me time' so that way I am not as drained by the time I get home. I have noticed that without these three hours of reading, meditation, exercise, writing or learning I am even more exhausted."

These are some awesome tips from John. Hopefully you find as much wisdom and help in his words as we have. Before we close out the chapter, we want to go over one last suggestion you can use to deal with the overstimulation of social situations.

One Final Tip…

Even if you're an introvert, you may have a job or other responsibilities that require you to be social. Since socializing can be so exhausting, it's crucial to schedule blocks of time to recharge your internal battery.

In her response to our survey, Honoree writes, *"The hardest thing I deal with is guarding my energy. I really do recharge alone, so attending multiple-day events or being around tons of people wears me out."*

Honoree's situation is a difficult one, particularly when it comes to feeling like she can't take the time to recharge.

If you have to attend a multi-day event, it helps to stay in your own room at the hotel where the event is being held, if your budget permits. If you have an on-site room and no roommate, you can go to your room for short periods of alone time without missing much of the event.

If possible, skipping an occasional session or spending part of the lunch break alone provides much-needed time to recharge.

Finally, it often pays to take a whole day off if you've had to socialize for many days in a row.

For example, right before starting this book, Rebecca attended a conference where she was surrounded by hundreds of people for a few days straight. Knowing this would wipe her out, and knowing she wanted to be in top form to start this book, she intentionally planned a "do nothing" day immediately following the conference. This time off helped her to recharge so she'd have the energy to focus on her next project.

Challenge #3: Being Perceived as Dull

As introverts, we often think carefully before speaking, so we have a tendency to not jump into fast-moving conversations. It's because of this quality that we often get labeled one (or all) of the following in a social situation:

- Cautious or hesitant
- Dull conversationalist
- Less interesting than other people

Sure, some introverts can be dull, just like some extroverts are dull. The problem is that people tend to label us "dull" or "uninteresting" simply because we are quiet by nature.

Perception vs. Reality

In spite of the fact that introverts are often perceived by others as being dull, many introverts are anything but. For example, Rebecca worked as an ethnographer in India, where she experienced everything from cooking her meals over an open fire in a village to having brunch with the Maharaja in his palace. When her children were young, they gave her the nickname "Hot Rod Mama."

Steve has also had his fair share of excitement. He's climbed Mt. Kilimanjaro, run 16 marathons and traveled to 30 countries, including an 8-month solo trip through Europe.

While it's highly unlikely that either Steve or Rebecca would ever do stand-up comedy, they both have a lot of interesting stories and insights to share when people get to know them.

And that's the rub. For people to see that you are anything but dull, they have to get to know you, which is a challenge for many introverts. Because introverts are less inclined to brag about their experiences than extroverts, many people don't take the time to get to know them.

Introverts Do Interesting Things (Quietly)

Some of the people who have contributed the most to the world have done so in very quiet ways.

Mahatma Gandhi comes to mind. You wouldn't expect a scrawny, bespectacled man in a loincloth who sat quietly spinning yarn to have a major impact on the world, but he did. In his own quiet way, he took on an entire empire and served as a great example of peaceful resistance for Martin Luther King, the Dalai Lama and others to follow.

Rosa Parks quietly refused to give up her seat on the bus and changed the course of history in a way that people will never forget.

Neither person had a flashy, boisterous personality, but each changed the course of history.

Not Boring. Not Dull. Just Different.

Introverts often have different ideas about how to have fun. For example, Audrey, one of Rebecca's former coworkers, once told her that people think she doesn't know how to have fun. As an introvert, Audrey thinks staying home and reading a good book is a fun activity.

Most introverts don't need to jump out of airplanes or practice extreme sports to be interesting or to have fun (although there are many introverts who love these activities).

Deep thinking and taking time to ponder serious issues, rather than just talking about "whatever," can be quite interesting if you take the time to share your thoughts with others.

Remember, introverts are:

- Writers
- Artists
- Deep thinkers
- People with vivid imaginations
- Scientists
- Philosophers

Anything that takes a little thought is right in the wheelhouse of the introvert.

In our opinion, these things are not boring at all, but far more interesting than talking about last night's sports scores or discussing other trivial items (although Steve enjoys these discussions as much he does the introspective activities).

The bottom line is that introverts don't have to become loud and flashy like their extroverted friends to be interesting. The key is to find an area of passion and explore it deeply; then find ways to share your interests with others.

The good news is we have a few tips on how to deal with the perception that introverts are dull.

Solutions for Challenge #3

Want to overcome a perception of dullness? If so, here is a four-step process for improving the impression people have about you.

Step 1: Don't worry about some people.

As painful as it may be, accept the fact that some people may think you're dull, even if you're not. Understand that this is their problem, and their loss, not yours. In our opinion, it's better to quickly recognize that you won't click with certain people than to waste time trying to win them over.

Step 2: Follow up with quality connections.

Many introverts struggle with being fast on their feet. Most of us think later, *"What I should have said. . ."* and wish we had thought of it during the actual conversation.

One way to deal with this is to follow up on the conversation with a short note or email that says something like, *"I really enjoyed the thoughts you shared about _____, especially _____.*

Or, *"Another way to look at this is_____."* (And then, of course, share your thoughts.)

Step 3: Embrace your interesting qualities.

Recognize that you may not be giving yourself enough credit. While you may feel that others think you're dull, and perhaps many people do, others may see that you are indeed an interesting person.

In response to our poll, Rachael wrote, *"Well-meaning extroverts tell me they enjoy having me around, and keep inviting me to things, but I think to myself, 'Why are you interested? I'm not like you; I'm not social.'"*

Rachael's comment is a good example of a "perception problem." Much of her uneasiness may come from an internal view that she is boring when the reality—people wanting her around—is just the opposite.

Step 4: Find your platform.

Demonstrate your expertise in quiet ways. For example, Steve and Rebecca write books.

Writing books may not be your cup of tea, but you may want to start a blog or join a forum. One reason that these options are great for introverts is that they give you the time to think through what you want to say.

Do your best to join online conversations so that people have a chance to get to know you. You may never be a fluid and graceful social conversationalist. Heck, you are an introvert; you can't (and shouldn't have to) change your stripes. However, you can be a little bit better at conversations if you practice and work on growing in this area.

The next few chapters give some ideas for the introvert looking to seem a bit more sociable.

The bottom line is that many introverts may be extra hard on themselves. They may feel like they are dull when they are not. They think they are boring because they don't have a billion things to say. The reality may be that, by listening and only speaking when there is something important to say, you will be viewed as wise and caring rather than dull.

Challenge #4: Lack of Confidence and Shyness

Another incorrect perception of introverts is that we lack confidence. However, as we've discussed before, it's silly to place a single label on an entire group of people. Yes, there are unconfident introverts, just as there are unconfident extroverts. The unfortunate reason we've gained this label is due to how we're often perceived in social situations.

So let's talk about the confidence label before we move on to the strategies you can use to build your self-esteem (if this is an area where you struggle).

It's All a Matter of Perception

First off, there's a difference between *feeling* confident and *looking* confident.

As we've already mentioned, in this extrovert-centric culture, the appearance of confidence is a quality many people desire. But we don't always get the whole story when you see someone demonstrating outgoing behavior.

For example, let's say you see a woman who boldly gets up and dances on a table. Perhaps you perceive her as someone who is confident. The reality, though, is maybe she's had too much to drink. Or perhaps she feels insecure and, since much of her sense of worth comes from gaining the attention of others, to build herself up, she dances on the tabletop.

The key factor to keep in mind is that perception and reality are two different things, and a confident introvert often looks *very* different than a confident extrovert.

The Confident Introvert

Think back to the 16 personalities test. If you looked at the different personality types, you saw there are introverts who are completely confident in themselves, yet they choose to be quiet, simply because they don't see the value of bombarding others with pointless small talk. These people are what we call "confident introverts."

Steve would consider himself to be a confident introvert. He's not the focal point at most social gatherings; instead, he's happiest when talking to a small group of people. His quiet nature isn't due to any sort of insecurity, but a lack of desire to be in the spotlight.

As a confident introvert, you know you are confident and have nothing to prove to others. You may even be quiet because you are confident. Rebecca has always loved a scripture verse that says, *"In quietness and confidence shall be your strength"* (Isaiah 30:15) because it pairs two unlikely things: quietness and confidence. When you pair the two on a daily basis, you'll see that it's possible to have a high level of self-esteem without feeling the need to be the most outgoing person in the room.

Don't view your quietness as weakness. It can actually be a *strength*. In fact, when you listen and only speak when you provide helpful thoughts, you will be viewed as wise. People will actually listen to what you have to say because they know you don't waste your breath speaking for the sake of speaking. You don't talk to show off. You're someone who speaks only when you have something important to say. That's the essence of a confident introvert.

So to recap, confident introverts:

- Don't feel that constant need to speak.
- Say important things.
- Know how to listen.

- Are comfortable with themselves.
- Inspire trust.
- Can be great leaders.

How Introversion is Different from Shyness

It's important to understand that, while many introverts are also shy, shyness isn't necessarily a part of being an introvert.

In fact, if you are an introvert who also happens to be shy, you are not a "shy introvert." That category doesn't exist! A better way to describe it would be to say that you are shy <u>and</u> an introvert.

Another way to look at it is that introversion is a part of who you are. It doesn't come about as a result of external experiences, but rather it's hardwired into you and cannot be changed.

In contrast, social anxiety usually stems from negative experiences and, while it may be difficult to overcome, it *can be* changed.

Rebecca was actually very shy as a child. She remembers being too shy to ask her babysitter for a drink of water, and in her early school years, she would go days without saying a word to anyone outside her family. Thankfully, she grew out of that. She still cherishes her alone time, but she can converse pretty easily with people and even enjoys public speaking. Rebecca is no longer extremely shy, but she's definitely still an introvert.

In response to our poll, Danielle gave a good example of what it's like to deal with shyness and introversion. As a child, she was considered an introvert and had trouble speaking out in school. Since she entered adulthood, Danielle has gone back to school and worked on her shyness and fears, and now she feels a lot more comfortable speaking out.

She conquered her shyness and lack of confidence; being an introvert had little to do with it.

While you can't "fix" being an introvert (nor do we recommend you even try), shyness is something you can overcome with persistent effort. Even though the introvert side of you may not like it, it is important to practice talking to people.

Not All Introverts are Confident

While the assumption that introverts lack confidence is incorrect, it is true that quite a few lack some degree of confidence. Low self-esteem is a human condition that impacts both introverts and extroverts. In fact, extroverts are just as likely to have low confidence as introverts.

It really depends on what type of introvert you are, as certain types are more prone to having a low level of confidence. There are other factors, such as upbringing, that also impact your personal level of self-assurance or lack thereof.

The bottom line is that any introvert can have a healthy sense of self-assurance, even if they're very quiet.

Solutions to Challenge #4

If you lack in confidence, realize that this is *not* a part of being an introvert. You will need to take specific actions to build up your self-confidence. Here is a quick overview of how to do this:

Step #1: Understand your barriers to self-confidence.

In the same way that shyness can be overcome, a lack of self-confidence can also be remedied. The first step in overcoming a lack of confidence is to understand the following barriers that may keep you from being confident in yourself:

- Childhood issues
- Fear of failure
- Fear of rejection
- Not anticipating setbacks
- Doubting your abilities
- Worrying too much about what others think
- Blaming others and not working on your issues
- Going right past confidence to arrogance
- Fearing success (Yes, even fear of success can hold people back.)

You don't have to talk to a psychologist to figure out why you feel a certain way, but it does help to journal on a daily basis.

During one of these sessions, think back to a recent event when you felt a lack of confidence.

Examine the thoughts that went through your head. *Did they remind you of an event from the past? How did this make you feel? Does the idea of being outgoing trigger any painful memories?*

You'll find that the more you understand these feelings of anxiety, the more equipped you'll be to overcome them.

Step 2: Try new things.

At the risk of sounding trite, the best way to build confidence is to regularly push the boundaries of your confidence, including doing things that make you feel scared on the inside.

The simplest way to gain confidence is to put yourself into social situations with strangers. We suggest creating a daily habit where you strike up a conversation with three to five people.

It doesn't matter *what you say*; what's more important is that you begin a conversation with a stranger. Do this on a regular basis and, in a short amount of time, the idea of meeting new people will seem perfectly natural.

Step 3: Review reminders of your positive qualities.

Accept compliments and feel good when you've done something good. You may even want to create a "feel good folder" where you keep email, cards, and other snippets of communication filled with praise. Refer to it when you doubt your worth.

We've all had those moments where we obsess over failures, forgetting about the hundreds of times we've been successful. If you maintain a folder filled with positive reminders, you'll have a database to refer to when you need to remember the times you've made a positive impact on other people's lives.

Set aside a minute or two every morning to recall past successes, your unique skills, positive relationships and any steps you have taken to improve your life. Let these ideas guide you to more successes.

Step 4: Join Toastmasters (or similar groups).

A supportive group can help you learn to love public speaking, and when people respond positively to your speeches, it will boost your confidence. It will also reduce anxiety if you find yourself in situations where you have to get in front of people.

You can find out more about Toastmasters by going to the main website (http://toastmasters.com) and looking for a local club in your area.

Building confidence is an ongoing activity. You can't take a crash course over a weekend and expect to feel comfortable at all times. However, if you challenge yourself to connect with others on a daily basis, you'll discover it's not that hard to become comfortable when meeting and talking to new people. We'll expand on this in the next few sections.

Challenge #5: Making a Good First Impression

As the old adage goes, *"You never have a second chance to make a good first impression."*

Unfortunately, making a good first impression is an area where many introverts struggle. Sure, we can be very talkative once we get to know someone, but it's hard for many of us to make a positive initial connection with someone new.

Sadly, people are often judged by the very first things they say to others. This means that if your first impression isn't...*impressive*, then you could be limiting your level of happiness and success in life.

So even if you're uncomfortable with the idea of initiating conversations, it's still important to know how (and when) to "come out of your shell" in social situations.

You Don't Need to Be an Extrovert, But...

As we stated previously, you can't magically transform into an extrovert since introversion is an unchangeable part of your makeup. Besides that, introversion isn't a type of illness that needs to be cured. But there are times when it's advantageous to your career and personal life to behave in an outgoing manner. This doesn't mean you have to *like* it.

For instance, Verity wrote, *"The sad answer is that...many introverts will never be 'comfortable' in social situations. Maybe we should stop trying to be. We should do it because we have to get the things we need and want, but should not have to change ourselves. Do what you need to do socially, you can work on that, but do not worry if you never are 'comfortable' with it. You may never be."*

Verity has a great point here. You may never become comfortable in social situations, but it's important to put yourself out there because it can help you get what you want in life.

Now, let's go over a few ways you can make a great first impression during a social encounter.

Solutions to Challenge #5

There is a lot of advice when it comes to creating a positive first impression. Some say you should be yourself, while others recommend creating an elevator pitch about what you can offer to others. We recommend a simple strategy for confidently articulating your value while carefully listening to other people in the conversation.

The key is to not just stand there bragging about your accomplishments, but to be an active listener. You need to tune in to what others say, respond to them in a positive manner and ask questions.

If you keep others talking about themselves, they will come away feeling fantastic about themselves—and you. In fact, they may even feel that you're an incredibly fascinating person, even if you didn't say much!

You may need some private time to recharge your batteries after being social, but it is possible to engage people in conversation when you first meet them and maintain this connection for years to come.

Ultimately, as an introvert, it is up to you to decide whether the effort expended and any discomfort it may cause is worth it to you.

To implement these strategies, we recommend five steps to use during any social encounter.

Step 1: Smile.

Yes, this might seem like overly simplistic advice, but Steve has lost of count of the number of times he's met someone who had an unhappy scowl on their face. Honestly, the best piece of advice we can give is to smile when you meet someone for the first time.

When you smile, it shows others that you're happy. If you need help flashing a genuine smile, think about things you enjoy, not the uncomfortable way you feel when meeting new people.

Rebecca has a tendency to think of funny things at the oddest times, which means she frequently grins from ear to ear. As a result, people sometimes tell her she has a beautiful smile. If only they knew what an introvert she is!

Step 2: Make eye contact.

This can feel very uncomfortable for an introvert, even more so if you're also shy. The good news is that eye contact doesn't have to last long. In fact, it's odd to stare down someone during a conversation. So, when the other person looks away, this is a good cue for you to look away as well.

Step 3: Give a firm handshake.

A firm handshake can give off an air of confidence, even when you don't feel confident. If you're unsure about the "quality" of your handshake, here is a great Lifehacker article on the five mistakes that people make while shaking hands:
http://bit.ly/1zd4M0Z

Step 4: Focus on others.

As mentioned above, when you focus on others, you don't have to do much of the actual talking, and people will walk away from the conversation impressed by how friendly you are.

A timeless classic that emphasizes this strategy is *How to Win Friends and Influence People*. While this book was written almost 80 years ago, its core principles still apply to modern social interactions.

Step 5: Create an elevator speech.

An elevator speech is a short (7 to 15 seconds in social situations, 15 to 30 seconds in networking situations) spiel that includes the highlights of your life.

- Who are you?
- What things make you unique? (It's okay to be confident.)
- What's in it for them? This is something that might hook the interest of the other person.
- Something fun about yourself, or a bit of self-deprecating humor

As an introvert, it is likely this will feel forced and unnatural to you, and make you uncomfortable. Neither Steve nor Rebecca enjoy talking about themselves, but having an elevator pitch prepared helps to eliminate the awkward silence when first meeting someone.

Here's an example of an elevator pitch Steve uses:

"I'm an author of short books, primarily through Amazon.com, that specialize in habit development. It's a great business because it allows me the flexibility to control my schedule and enjoy my passions—like traveling."

Steve's elevator pitch is short and succinct. It's only two sentences long, but includes a few hooks (like publishing on Amazon and traveling the world) that can be used to seed the conversation.

Keep in mind that your elevator pitch doesn't have to be very long. It's simply a few sentences with a few threads that can be used to continue the conversation. Now, if you want to improve your introduction skills, we recommend these four methods for improving your elevator speech: http://bit.ly/1SdlrWI

Challenge #6: The Fine Art of Small Talk

Making a good first impression is only one *social* challenge that introverts face. In fact, many struggle with their first words because they don't know how to handle the next phase of the conversation—small talk.

It's not enough to get up the nerve to introduce yourself with an elevator speech. What you need to do next is know how to engage in small talk that leads to a fun conversation.

Why Small Talk Matters

As much as you might dislike small talk, you should recognize that it *is* a social ritual that's a normal part of everyday life. This means it's important to understand the fundamentals if you want to network, meet new people and build friendships.

As a person uncomfortable with small talk, Rebecca used to tell herself, "small talk is dumb" as justification for not even trying. Over time, she realized that small talk did serve an important function for the success of her business.

For instance, Rebecca knows that small talk makes her more likable, which can result in opportunities that come up less often for those who are more standoffish. Also, small talk is often the foundation for building relationships and having more substantial conversations down the road.

This realization made small talk more palatable and motivated Rebecca to get "good enough" at it to get by. While it's still not her favorite thing, she doesn't mind it as much as she used to, and on some occasions even enjoys it.

With that in mind, let's go over a few ways to improve your small-talk skills.

Solutions to Challenge #6

Simply put, the best way to improve your small talk is to practice it on a consistent basis.

Here is a seven-step process that can help you get started.

Step 1: Ask others about themselves.

Whenever possible, be the first to ask questions about the other person. The easiest thing to do is to look for "conversation threads," which are passing comments about a person's background or interests. Simply ask other people about one of these threads, and they will usually end up doing most of the talking.

That said, don't be afraid to talk about yourself and weave similar experiences into the conversation so you can find common ground. If you find yourself talking too much, simply turn the conversation back to the other person by just saying something like, *"What about you?"*

Step 2: Pay attention.

As introverts, we're good at noticing things but often fail to share our observations. So take notice and *share*. Compliment people you meet on things you notice and like: glasses, clothes, hats, ties, shoes, jewelry, shirts, etc. Remember that everyone loves a compliment. Just be sure to be genuine, because people can small flattery a mile away, and most are turned off by it.

Another way to get someone to talk is to incorporate your immediate surroundings and talk about them.

For example, whenever Steve gets a haircut, he'll often joke around with the stylist (because he doesn't enjoy having a stranger in his personal space for an extended period of time.)

So if the waiting area is really crowded and the stylist looks stressed, he'll say, *"I see you're having a nice relaxing day at work."*

Or if it's really quiet, he'll say, *"I can see you're having a busy day today."*

Yes, these seem like silly comments, but what they do is get the stylist to start talking about her day or her job. From there, the small talk flows pretty easily.

Step 3: Add "meat" to the conversation.

Many introverts hate small talk because it's often filled with pointless fluff. Rather than conform to this standard, try to make meaningful and significant connections with the other person. Your goal is to make a connection to a person's passion. Try discussing the following topics:

- The other person's job
- Hobbies (athletic or nonathletic)
- Lifestyle
- Travel
- Dreams and aspirations

What you talk about really depends on the person. For instance, some people love talking about their jobs, while others don't want to discuss this topic. Our suggestion is to talk about different things until you can tell the other person seems to really respond to the topic.

The key here is to express interest while avoiding the 20-question interrogation. Ask a few questions to get things going, but don't monopolize the conversation. Try to have a normal conversation where you go back and forth talking about your experiences.

Step 5: Practice verbal Kung Fu.

Again, one of the keys to small talk is to avoid the trap of carrying the conversation on your own. A great way to do this is to practice active listening. If you're unfamiliar with active listening, think about a psychologist you may have seen on TV (or in real life). They listen and ask pertinent questions such as, *"How did you feel about that?"* and *"What did you do next?"* to keep the other person talking.

In response to our poll, Jon S. wrote, *"I practice making connections. When I'm going to an outgoing event, I often figure out questions to ask of particular people so I can have something to talk about. This works for family reunions, work parties, and even neighborhood gatherings. Facebook is particularly helpful. It allows us to start in the middle of the conversation."*

Step 6: Don't worry about being an expert.

When you have no experience in a topic, don't present yourself as an expert. Instead, be honest about your lack of knowledge and give people an opportunity to teach you something new.

Yes, sometimes this means you end up talking about a topic that does not interest you at all. Perhaps you even think it's a silly subject, but if it interests the other person, then use the conversation as an opportunity to learn more about it.

For instance, Steve knows nothing about basketball, yet when someone brings up the topic, he simply asks questions and has the other person do the talking. He hasn't watched a full basketball game in the last decade, but he knows a good amount about the sport, simply because it's a topic he often discusses with the people he meets.

Step 7: Discuss boring topics sparingly.

When all else fails, resort to talking about subjects that everyone has in common, such as the weather or the latest football game. News stories, especially ones with local interest, are also safe, so long as they aren't political or religious in nature.

Now, these seven steps barely scratch the surface of engaging people with small talk. If you'd like to learn more, we suggest two books: *How to Win Friends and Influence People* by Dale Carnegie and *Speak Up: The Introvert's Guide to Confidence, Friends, and Conquering Anxiety* by Patrick King (who is a prolific author specializing in the topic of dating and social skill development).

Challenge #7: Talking on the Phone

Another challenge many introverts face is talking on the phone.

Sara W. writes: *"I absolutely hate it when the telephone rings in my home. I am terrified of answering it. I feel like a phone ringing is an invasion of peace and desired solitude."*

Sara isn't the only person to feel this way. Great dislike (or even a fear) of the phone came up multiple times in our survey. For many of us, talking on the phone can be more draining than speaking to small groups of people and engaging in face-to-face conversations.

For instance, Imad F. said the following:

"You would think as someone who doesn't like social interaction, I would prefer talking on the phone to a face to face conversation. But I'm quite the opposite. I hate having to dial the phone to talk to anyone for any reason. Unless it's my family members."

We totally get this response.

Here are a few reasons why many introverts despise talking on the phone.

Reason 1: Phone conversations often include small talk.

We've already touched upon the dislike that many introverts have for small talk, but for many, it's even worse on the phone. The whole point of some phone calls is to make small talk instead of discussing any one topic in depth. This is especially true if you live in the southern part of the United States (where most folks have a relaxed way of living).

For instance, when Rebecca first moved to a small town in Texas, she learned the hard way how important it is to spend the first several minutes of a phone call on random chit-chat before getting into the real reason for the call. She recalls a time when she started a phone conversation with a friend in her typical "Southern California style." After briefly asking the recipient of the call how she was, Rebecca immediately launched into, "The reason I'm calling is…" and got right to the point of the phone call.

After the call had ended, her friend called her back to see "if anything was wrong" and if Rebecca was mad at her. Why? Because Rebecca spent too little time on idle chit-chat.

This cultural aspect of the town made phone calls even more draining. Regardless of where you live, at least some small talk is almost guaranteed to be a part of any phone conversation.

Reason #2: You can't read body language.

It's impossible to gauge the subtle nuances of a conversation while you're on the phone. Since 90 percent of our conversation is done on the nonverbal level, it's easy to miss important cues. Perhaps the other person is bored or dislikes what you're saying, but you often don't see that because there are no physical signals to pick up on. Overall, all of this can be exasperating to someone (like your average introvert) who doesn't like phone conversations in the first place.

Reason #3: Phone conversations are often inconvenient.

For many of us, phone calls often seem like an intrusion that interrupts the flow of whatever we're doing at the time. Many introverts are deep thinkers and also enjoy a certain amount of order, and phone calls disrupt both things.

Calls always seem to come at "a bad time," unless they are scheduled in advance. This is particularly true for introverts who feel that *any* time is a bad time for the phone to ring. Also, since phone calls often come at unexpected times, you never know who may call or when. There is no way to prepare for unexpected calls ahead of time, which can be nerve-wracking for introverts.

Reason #4: It's hard to end some conversations.

It can be hard to gracefully end a phone conversation. Someone has to decide that the conversation is over, and it can be hard for an introvert to be assertive enough to be the one to make that move.

For instance, Rebecca once ended up spending three painful hours on the phone with a friend because the friend simply wouldn't stop talking, and Rebecca couldn't figure out a way to nicely end the call.

Okay, we've covered four reasons why phone conversations can be a painful experience for many introverts. That said, it is important to learn ways to manage calls for those times when you absolutely have to talk on the phone.

Solutions for Challenge #7

You should treat phone conversations as a form of small talk. Start with a few pleasantries before diving into the focus of the conversation. How much time you spend on pleasantries really depends on the person you're talking to, the urgency of what you need and how much time you have to talk. The key here is to approach the phone conversation in a relaxing manner instead of speeding ahead to the end result.

Here are six strategies we recommend:

Strategy #1: Screen your calls.

Determine ahead of time who you will always take phone calls from, and then choose to screen the other calls.

For instance, Rebecca has decided that she always has time to talk to her 83-year-old mom. Since her mom is elderly and lives in another state, Rebecca understands the value of those conversations, so she chats even when she's not in the mood to do so. Needless to say, she screens calls from other people, who may not have anything urgent to discuss.

Strategy #2: Let most calls go to voicemail.

This puts you in control of the situation, which eases some of the stress. You can listen to the messages at your leisure and respond in a way that is more comfortable for you. For instance, unless it's necessary to call the person back, you may respond to their voicemail via text, email or private Facebook messages.

Strategy #3: Have more than one phone number.

If you're in a job that requires a lot of phone conversations, then you should consider having a private phone number that you only give to people in your inner circle.

Some Android and Windows phones have slots for dual SIM cards, which makes it easy to have two phone numbers on a single phone. If your phone doesn't have that capability, you can give your actual phone number to a small group of people and use a Skype or Google Voice phone number for everyone else.

Strategy #4: Use technology to filter your calls.

Many phones (like the Windows phone) allow you to set up an inner circle and then set rules about calls and texts coming from people outside of that circle. You do need to have a plan for getting back to people outside of your inner circle, but you can do so in your own time.

Strategy #5: Get to the point.

If phone calls make you feel particularly anxious, then immediately get to what you (or the other person) need; then end the conversation fairly quickly.

As Rebecca mentioned above, this is more difficult in certain cultures. No matter where you live, people can learn that you don't mean to be rude by keeping conversations short. Yes, this won't make you the best phone conversationalist in the world, but it *will* reduce a lot of stress.

Strategy #6: Use time blocks for your phone conversations.

Set aside one day per week for scheduled phone appointments. For instance, both Rebecca and Steve schedule all podcast interviews and other phone appointments for Wednesday. While this makes it an exhausting day, they avoid talking on the phone for the rest of the week.

We admit that some of these strategies might seem a little impersonal. They might even seem counterintuitive to Challenge #1, which talks about overcoming the perception of being rude.

Our point? If you currently avoid the phone so much that it's having a negative impact on your life, it's okay to use these strategies. They'll be helping you overcome an obstacle.

Challenge #8: Building Relationships

Once first impressions and small talk are over, the next hurdle for introverts is developing those long-term relationships, including romantic, friendly and business relationships.

Think Quality Instead of Quantity

There is nothing wrong with only having a small group of close friends. Understand that, as an introvert, you may not have hundreds of acquaintances and casual friendships, but you really a few to have a fulfilled life.

Both Rebecca and Steve suggest that it's far better to focus on a small number of quality relationships. Don't feel bad about having a limited circle of friends. Be proud that your interactions tend to be deep and meaningful.

This quote by an anonymous author sums it up nicely:

"True friendship multiplies the good in life and divides its evils. Strive to have friends, for life without friends is like life on a desert island. To find one real friend in a lifetime is good fortune:

To keep him is a blessing."

Friendships are indeed important, and life without any friends is unhealthy. We all need other people. But focus on true friends, real friends that you can have for life. Don't feel like you are somehow less valuable than someone who seemingly has hundreds of friends.

Remember, if you have even one real friend in a lifetime, you're wealthy in a way that money or fame could never provide.

Conflicts in Relationships Are Inevitable

Few people enjoy conflict, but introverts may be even more averse to conflict than their extroverted friends.

Unfortunately, different personalities and goals for relationships can lead to conflict. This is especially true in relationships between introverts and extroverts, and we'll cover how to deal with that in Challenge #13.

Regardless of personality type, know that to some degree, conflicts in relationships are inevitable. Don't beat yourself up over them when they happen. Instead, strive to be at peace with those who matter the most to you. Remember to focus on quality relationships with a few, rather than trying to get along with everyone.

Now the question is:

"How do I build those quality relationships that last a lifetime?"

In the following section, we go over a few core strategies for creating the type of interactions that stand the test of time.

Solutions to Challenge #8

There are four strategies to not only improve the quality of your relationships, but to also enhance any future connections you make.

Strategy 1: Understand what you want.

It is important that both people in any relationship (romantic, friendly and business) know what they ultimately want.

Both sides have to bend. That means you might need to spend time being social when you might prefer being alone. But that also means that the other person needs to compromise and understand that you *need* occasional alone time or that you enjoy more one-on-one conversation.

Once you clearly know what you want from your relationships, you can begin to search actively for people who fit that mold.

Strategy 2: Let others see the real you.

If you put on a persona that is not "you" with new relationships, you are deceiving others. They are not seeing and befriending who you are, but who you are pretending to be. This leads to a dilemma. At some point you will need to come clean and let them know what you actually enjoy, or you will remain miserable because you're trying to be someone you are not.

We feel that the more authentic you are with the people you meet, the easier time you will have attracting equally genuine people who enjoy being with you as you are.

Strategy 3: Set relationship boundaries.

Relationship boundaries are not intended to hold others separate or "away." They are a way to keep a relationship healthy and natural.

For introverts, setting these boundaries may be as simple as letting others know that, while you enjoy their company, you need some time alone from time to time to recharge your batteries.

Be honest. Let others know what you enjoy, what you can tolerate and what you hate.

The truth can be sexy!

Strategy 4: Let go of toxic relationships.

Some relationships are more draining than others, and some can even be devastating, particularly if the other party seems bent on tearing you down. Whenever possible, walk away from those relationships, and use your renewed energy to work on the relationships that really matter.

If the toxic relationship is with a family member, you might need to maintain some level of the relationship, but you should also avoid this person as much as you can.

These steps might seem overly simplistic, but they are a good starting point for surrounding yourself with people who uplift you. We only have a limited amount of time on this earth, so you might as well focus on spending time with the people who truly get you.

Challenge #9: Being Pushed Around

Pam writes: "Pushy people assume that because I am an introvert that I can be pushed around. When they push, and I eventually enforce my personal boundaries, they actually become angry with me for doing so. Very irritating and a waste of my time."

There are times when the quiet nature of introverts is misconstrued as weakness. Even worse, some people assume that the supposedly weak introverts can be pushed around. This perception is, unfortunately, reinforced whenever you allow others to bully you.

In some ways, it's not surprising that bullying happens to introverts. After all, it often seems that "he who shouts loudest is heard the best." Being loud isn't something that introverts are known for, and because of it, their opinions and wishes are often overlooked.

One thing that stood out to us in Pam's quote (shared above) are the words, "When they push and I **eventually** enforce my personal boundaries, they actually become angry with me for doing so."

The word "eventually" is a key to understanding why this happens. As introverts, we are often slow to speak up, enforce boundaries and make a stand for what we believe. Because of this, we inadvertently condition pushy people to take advantage of us.

That's the bad news. The good news is that books such as *Quiet* by Susan Cain are helping to change the perception that introverts are nothing more than spineless wallflowers. Unfortunately, some of the worst offenders (including people introverts rub shoulders with on a regular basis) haven't read that book and may not be tuned in to much of anything when it comes to how introverts think and feel.

What is also good news is that it doesn't have to be that way. Even as an introvert, you can, in your own quiet way, stand up to pushy people.

The section below provides solutions for bringing about this change in your own world.

Solutions to Challenge #9

Here are six ways to structure your relationships so that you can set boundaries, prevent yourself from being pushed around and set the tone for future relationships with the people around you.

Step 1: Determine your core values.

What things matter most in your life? Is it your family? Health? Finances?

This is different for everyone, so there are no right or wrong answers to this question. As you'll see in the next step, it's important to think this through carefully.

Step 2: Choose your battles.

It's important to determine *where* you want to stand firm and what truly doesn't matter. By standing your ground on the important things (and letting everything else slide), you will invest your energy in the areas that can have the most positive impact on your life.

In other words, you should focus on fighting for your core values.

For example, if one of your core values is time with family, and you have a demanding boss that wants you to work late, then create a personal policy to leave the office by a certain time and avoid working on weekends. You can make exceptions to your policy if you have to finish a mandatory project.

With defined core values, you'll know which battles to fight and when it's appropriate to compromise.

Step 3: Communicate your non-negotiables.

It's important to set proper expectations for those who may have a tendency to run all over you.

With the example in step two, you would need to have a conversation with your boss about your decision to make family a priority. Explain that, unless it's an emergency, you won't be able to work late. Having the talk ahead of time will make it easier to stick to your guns the next time someone asks you to violate your core values.

Step 4: Speak up.

Another big challenge introverts face is not speaking up when we should. We often let people walk all over us when it's important to say something.

Our advice is simple. If you want people to respect your opinion and boundaries, then you need to say something to anyone who violates one of your core values.

Step 5: Put it in writing.

If you really find it hard to speak up, write out what you have to say in a note or email, and send your thoughts. This will give you time to figure out what needs to be said without getting tongue-tied or being intimidated by a potentially confrontational conversation.

When you write to someone, you need to do so in a way that acknowledges the other person's value and opinion, and explains why you must take a stand on a particular issue.

Step 6: Decide where to compromise.

This is the flip side of choosing your battles, and it helps to keep things in balance. Let's say that one of the battles you've chosen to fight is to leave work on time so you can spend time with your family. That's a great area to take a stand, but there may be times you need to compromise.

For example, your workplace may have a big annual event, and in order to pull it off, everyone has to work late. Or perhaps there's quarterly inventory, and again, everyone in the company has to work late.

Yielding in these areas shows that you're a team player, and it will go a long way toward helping your boss be understanding during those times when you have to take a stand.

Challenge #10: Working in Teams

When it comes to workplace trends, things are moving in a less introvert-friendly direction. It used to be that terms such as "employees" or "staff" were common. While those terms are still used, "team" has become a common term to describe people who work at a company, or in a specific department.

This is more than just a change in terminology. It's a change in how many businesses operate. Now more than ever, projects have a team focus, which means that rather than working mostly alone on assigned tasks, almost everything is a group effort.

Many companies now have open-concept offices where walls (even in the form of cubicles) don't exist. And of course, there are those popular team-building exercises that make most introverts cringe.

All of these changes in the workplace cause a lot of anxiety and, in many cases, result in lower performance from and less recognition of introverts.

For instance, Kevin Cheng wrote, *"If I had a dime for every time in my life I've thought of relevant, decent insights or ideas that would have added value to an earlier conversation, but AFTER the fact so no one really knew I had all that potential to contribute. And sometimes I'd lose the opportunity to work on something that I'm truly qualified for and interested in doing."*

He went on to say, *"We introverts are never totally relaxed in the presence of others (aside from our family and close friends). So part of my mind is preoccupied just dealing with this nervous tension, so I don't think of those nice ideas/solutions when I'm in a live meeting or brainstorming session, but I do afterwards when I'm alone, totally relaxed."*

Also, Patrik wrote, *"It's difficult to have people understand that I cannot always provide an answer to whatever it is just like that. I need some time to think. If they stress me I will only provide the answers I think they want to hear. And that's not always quality."*

The bottom line is that, while introverts can work in teams, our best contributions often come about as a result of alone time. We do better when we have time to formulate an answer. When given time, our answers are often more thoughtful, reasoned, researched and just plain "better" than those of our extrovert brethren who may have a quick reply ready on any given topic.

We also tend to get a lot more done when working alone than when working in a group.

The solutions below will help you know how to be a team player, even if you'd rather sit in a corner alone.

Solutions to Challenge #10

Here are four strategies to successfully work in teams while giving yourself enough alone time to work on important projects.

Strategy 1: Make sure people understand your quirks.

Kevin Cheng has a great suggestion for laying the foundation when working with teams:

"I suggest an introvert tell everyone outright in a meeting or group setting that often their best ideas and answers come after the meeting. There should be a way to ask for and agree on a way to follow up with the decision-maker afterwards.

This has dropped my nervous tension a ton, because I don't feel 'under pressure' to speak up right then and there or else forever hold my peace. Ironically, in my now more relaxed state, I often am able to contribute more effectively during the meeting as well."

Everyone has their own particular way of communicating. If you're someone who thinks better in isolation, then be honest with other team members. Tell them you don't always work best in a team setting, but you <u>will</u> follow up each meeting with a number of ideas after you've had time to think. A simple follow-up email filled with suggestions can be a nice way to tie together what was discussed at a meeting, while providing a fresh perspective on the topic.

Strategy 2: Find "introverted" ways to contribute to team efforts.

Even with team projects, there are things that can be done alone. For example, Rebecca has volunteered to drive to the rec center to pick up items for the company picnic. This gave her some alone time, and no one else had to be bothered with the rather menial task. She also became the person in her department to edit all written communication, which required time alone at her desk.

Strategy 3: Suggest a ROWE (Results-Oriented Work Environment).

Kimberly Schimmel wrote, *I am a fan of ROWE (Results-Oriented Work Environment) instead of herding people into cubicles on a precise schedule.*

Here are the basic components of ROWE:

1. As the name implies, the focus is on results, not on the time spent on a project.
2. There are clearly defined goals and expectations.
3. Results are directly rewarded financially, and through job security.
4. It takes the nebulous "social" aspects out of a work environment.
5. Conversations focus on what needs to be done.
6. Everyone is held accountable for what is done.

ROWE is not something for every job or every situation, but it is something that (if given the chance) most introverts could excel at.

If you're in a position of authority (even if it's leading a team of just a few people), you can implement ROWE. If you're not in a position of authority, present the idea to your boss and/or HR manager. For more on ROWE, feel free to check out Kimberly's article on the subject: http://bit.ly/1HkfWma

Strategy #4: Request an alternate work environment.

When Rebecca still worked a full-time job, due to multiple interruptions throughout the day, she found it hard to get work done. She came up with a plan that included working in a "hidden" office one day per week, and presented the idea to her boss and the HR director. She assured them this would enable her to be more productive.

They approved the plan on a trial basis, and when Rebecca's productivity shot through the roof, they made it permanent.

For this to work, keep the following in mind:

- Prove yourself ahead of time. The approval Rebecca received was largely based on her proven track record as a conscientious employee.
- Work within company policies. For instance, Rebecca's employer didn't allow people to work from home. Her solution worked within those confines since she was still on the premises on her "alone" days.
- Provide a logical and well thought-out plan for why an alternative work environment benefits the company.
- Suggest that it be done on a trial basis, with a scheduled follow-up evaluation. It's easier to get higher-ups to approve something that is temporary.
- Go out of your way to do a good job during the trial basis, and document the results.
- In the follow-up meeting, present the documentation of what you were able to accomplish as a result of the alternate work environment.

The key with an alternate work proposal is that you keep the needs of the company front and center. Doing so provides a win not just for you, but for the company as well.

Working in a team-focused environment doesn't have to be a daunting challenge for an introvert. Simply follow these four steps to learn how to contribute in a meaningful manner while maintaining the flexibility to work in a solitary manner so you can focus on delivering top-notch work.

Challenge #11: Giving Feedback

Many introverts struggle with giving feedback to others, particularly when it's negative.

For example, have you ever had a co-worker, boss, or even a friend say or do something that you really didn't like and even when it made sense to tell them about it, you kept quiet instead? Or perhaps you denied there was a problem, even when you were specifically asked about it.

You may do this out of fear or shyness, or due to a lack of confidence.

Regardless of the reason, many introverts are by nature non-confrontational, and while avoiding conflict may seem like a good thing, it can cause a lot of problems down the road.

For example, without giving feedback, you may find yourself in a situation where you're stuck doing something you hate. Additionally, if you don't address problems directly, you can start resenting other people and quickly hit your breaking point.

If you're in a position of authority and let things slide with a subordinate, tasks may go unfinished or work won't be completed to a satisfactory level.

Letting things slide isn't fair to everyone in your business. It's not fair to the employer who expects you to make sure the work gets done correctly. It's not fair to other team members who may have to pick up the slack to make up for the person who isn't doing a good job. As strange as it may seem, it's not even fair to the subordinate who isn't performing as well as you'd like. You don't want them shocked when they receive a bad review, get passed over for a promotion, or even worse, end up jobless.

The bottom line is that it's important to speak up when something isn't quite right.

Solution to Challenge #11

Providing feedback to others isn't always easy to do, but here are eight steps to make it as painless as possible.

Step 1: Be honest with yourself.

Sometimes an adverse reaction to a negative experience can be the result of a personality conflict. Let's be honest here...sometimes you will work with people you simply don't like. The problem is, even if you don't like someone, you still have to be as professional as possible and find a way to work together in a professional manner.

This means it's important to at least consider the source of any irritation or negative feelings you might have about the person before moving forward with the rest of these steps.

Step 2: Plan out your feedback.

Since introverts tend to do a better job at most everything if they've been given time to think things through, then you should avoid giving feedback on the fly. Instead, take the time to think through the issue and jot down some notes.

If you're pressed for feedback by someone else, ask for permission to think it through and set a time to get back to the person.

Step 3: Ask permission.

If someone isn't open to receiving feedback, then it's almost guaranteed that things won't go well if you forge on ahead. In that case, the feedback won't achieve the desired outcome and may even backfire and impact the relationship in a negative way. Getting permission ahead of time helps smooth things over and increases the odds of a positive outcome.

Step 4: Commit yourself.

If you're concerned that you'll wimp out and not give feedback, do something that will make it hard to back out. For example, let the person know that you have some feedback for them and ask to set up an appointment to discuss it.

Step 5: Criticize in private.

No one likes to be made to look foolish in front of other people. Show proper respect by giving feedback in private.

Step 6: Don't stockpile negatives.

One problem many introverts have when it comes to giving feedback is that they avoid doing so until the pressure builds to the point of frustration. If you do this, and let it rip, the recipient of your feedback will feel under attack. Often a conversation like this can turn ugly, so our advice is to speak up about an important issue sooner rather than later.

If you've let things build, pick the primary issue that needs to be addressed, and focus only on that. The other things can be dealt with later!

Step 7: Be specific about the changes you want to see.

When you present the problem, be sure also to offer a solution to the problem. Be specific so that the person receiving the criticism isn't left wondering what to do next.

Step 8: Treat others like you want to be treated.

We saved this step for last because it's crucial for all of the other steps to work well. Put yourself in the other person's shoes, and act in a way that you would prefer if you were the one receiving feedback.

Be honest, but kind. Listen to the other person's point of view. Be fair, and take responsibility for your actions if you contributed to the problem. Don't vent, blow off steam or attack in any other way. Remember, even if you're frustrated with the person, you gain more by confronting with kindness than you ever will by attacking.

Challenge #12: Not Having Your Contributions Recognized

As an introvert, you may prefer to stay in the background. While the background might be a comfortable place, staying there can have a disastrous impact on your career and personal life. Your contributions might go unnoticed, and in some cases, others may reap the financial rewards for your hard work.

We received an email in response to our poll that illustrates the problem perfectly.

Eileen wrote,

"...When I was a fledgling attorney and an introvert (I know, an oxymoron, 'introverted attorney') no matter how good my work was or my idea, someone else took credit for it. I learned early on to stay in the background and focus on the things I loved, like client one-on-one interfacing and legal research. My documents were impeccable, but someone else argued them in court or other public forums. This was all right with me because I felt like a key part of the team. Except no one EVER gave me credit.

I realize now that this was very damaging to my career track. I should have learned how to take credit. One glaring example was a case where we represented a public agency being sued by another public agency. Our office was about to offer settlement (hundreds of thousands of dollars) when my research turned up an obscure water resource law that completely exonerated our client. My boss took my documents to negotiations, and the lawsuit was dropped. As a result, he got a huge bonus and large retainer from our client.

My work was never acknowledged. An extrovert would not have tolerated this."

In presenting ideas in any public forum, even a volunteer group, an introvert's idea is often overlooked or ignored until the same idea is presented by an extrovert, who offers it with more enthusiasm or razzle-dazzle. It is no wonder introverts become more introverted as time goes on. But they are great on one-man projects.

Eileen's story illustrates a couple of great points.

First, even in a job that tends to be geared toward extroverts (like practicing law), there is room for introverts just to be introverts and do excellent work.

Second, staying in the background in a career like this can often keep you from getting ahead. While it is not natural for introverts to force credit upon themselves, sometimes it's something *you have to do* even if it makes you feel uncomfortable. If you're unwilling to fight for the credit you deserve, chances are, you'll be left behind as others get attention for the hard work that you put in.

Besides not having your contributions be recognized, there are five specific challenges introverts face when it comes to the work environment.

#1. Struggles with self-promotion

Generally speaking, most introverts don't like to talk about themselves. As an introvert, you're likely not the type to sit around and brag about what you've done!

The problem? While humility is great, if you want the credit you deserve (plus the benefits that come with), it's important to ring your own bell. If you're not willing to do some self-promotion, then don't expect others to do it for you.

#2. Dislike for being in the spotlight or asking for testimonials

We feel you on this one. Steve often feels very awkward asking for testimonials. In fact, when he considers asking for testimonials from his readers, self-doubt rushes in and he often even fears that they might not be as happy with the content as he hoped.

As an introvert, not liking these things is part of who you are, and because of that, it won't change. But it's like eating your vegetables. You may not like it, but as an adult you have to do it anyway if you want your career to grow up strong and healthy.

#3. Preference for avoiding confrontation

We dealt with this in the last chapter, but it's worth addressing again here because this tendency is what allows people to publicly take credit, and in some cases the rewards, for our hard work.

Rebecca shared one of her best ideas with one of her clients, a well-known thought leader in her industry. He liked the idea and had her flesh it out. She poured hours of time and lot of creativity into the project.

When Rebecca finished her hard work, and it was time to launch this new service, her client went out of his way to explain how he came up with the idea. He didn't mention Rebecca's contribution, or the fact that she had the original idea and did every bit of the work developing the concept.

Rebecca felt betrayed by his actions, and as she listed to the praise he received for "his" great idea, the hurt went even deeper. But she didn't say anything until months later. This ultimately damaged her relationship, and she no longer works for him.

#4. Failure to speak up

This problem often comes about because introverts tend to stay out of the spotlight and avoid confrontation.

While it's unnatural for introverts to stand up and claim their ideas, it's important to take that stand. If you let others get away with co-opting your work, without taking at least a few small steps for self-promotion, then you have to accept at least a share of the blame yourself.

#5. Success stories often center on extroverts.

As a society (especially in the United States) we love stories of scrappy, personable visionaries who can easily articulate the missions of their businesses. The downside is that the equally important, but less vocal, introvert is sometimes shunted aside or forgotten.

A good example is Steve Jobs and Steve Wozniak. As the extrovert, Jobs' name is synonymous with Apple, and he gets sole credit for the success of Apple, but Woz was just as important as Jobs in the early days of the company. In later years, Jobs even hired thousands of "Woz-type" introverts to execute his dreams.

Solutions to Challenge #12

It's not all doom-and-gloom for the introvert when it comes to getting proper credit at work. In fact, you don't have to be the most outspoken person in to receive recognition. All you have to do is follow the seven steps we've outlined below.

Step 1: Recognize that "self-promotion" isn't a bad thing.

While no one wants to be around arrogant people who are always tooting their own horns, it's not wrong, selfish or prideful to speak up for yourself when it's appropriate to do so.

Step 2: Understand that timing is critical.

Self-promote sparingly. Once a month in a work environment is enough for people to see your contribution, but not so often that it's offensive or annoying.

Keep your self-promotion to the topics at hand. For example, when Rebecca's client took credit for her idea, the idea was discussed in a team meeting. At that time, it made sense to mention how the idea originated and what worked in building the plan. Naturally, it's important to do this in a way that doesn't publicly disgrace the person who took credit.

Step 3: Focus on getting tangible results from your efforts.

Rather than using vague terms like, "XYZ turned out really well," say something like, "After we implemented XYZ, we had ABC results that lead to [name specific outcome]."

While qualitative information is helpful, be sure to include quantitative results whenever possible.

Step 4: Use meetings to showcase your knowledge.

Speaking up in meetings can be tough for introverts. To make it easier, plan in advance what you're going to say. In fact, if it makes sense to do so, put together a nice-looking document and make copies of it for all attendees.

If you know the meeting agenda ahead of time and have good ideas that fit with the agenda, let your boss know that you have something to share with the group. Just before the meeting, share the document you prepared with your boss and ask if you can briefly present it during the meeting.

Step 5: Document your accomplishments.

Don't just say you are "the best;" show your boss your work and effort, and let those things be the deciding factor in determining your value to the business.

One way to go about this is to document the things you do, including courses you take, projects you work on and certifications you've received. Even better—keep a timeline of these specific career milestones. Have this information on hand for performance reviews.

This is a tactic that can be carried out quietly, and yet it's impressive to have a whole list of what you accomplished.

Step 6: Have a heart-to-heart conversation with any offenders.

Rather than making a public scene or letting it get under your skin, pull the boss or co-worker aside and let them know your feelings. They may not be intentionally trying to back-stab you; they may think they are just sharing ideas from a collaborative environment.

If the heart-to-heart conversation doesn't go well, it could be a sign that you need to look for another place of employment.

Step 7: Share your new ideas publicly first.

Many introverts aren't crazy about speaking up in public and may bounce ideas off of others before sharing them publicly. Some sleazy co-workers or bosses may use these opportunities to co-opt your ideas and present them as their own. While this may spare you from the need to speak up in the meeting, if you don't introduce the idea yourself, others may get the recognition or promotion you deserve.

If you share the ideas publicly, others will (hopefully) remember that you were the one with the idea and back you when others take credit.

If you initially share your ideas one-on-one, follow up the chat with an email that summarizes the conversation. Do it in a non-confrontational and positive way. For instance, you can start off by thanking the person for listening to and giving you feedback on your idea.

When it makes sense to do so, include your boss in the correspondence. You may even write directly to the manager and copy the person with whom you shared the idea. Just be sure to do this in a way that is upbeat, has a clear reason for including the boss, and appropriately gives the other person credit where credit is due.

Challenge #13: Nurturing Relationships with Extroverts

People say that opposites attract, and that is often the case with introverts and extroverts. This attraction can be true in friendships *and* love. For example, it's not uncommon for an introvert to marry an extrovert. On top of that, introverts may have extroverted children, siblings or other family members and friends.

This attraction is a good thing because there are positive and negative traits to each personality type. When you put the two together, you often have a balance that wouldn't be possible if two introverts or two extroverts got together.

That said, even in the most balanced of relationships, sometimes there can be conflicts, especially when you're dealing with the different ways introverts and extroverts like to communicate.

In this chapter, we'll deal with some of the challenges that come with living with spouses and other family members (or roommates) who are extroverted. These same principles will help you navigate relationships with your extroverted friends.

Specifically, there are three challenges you've probably encountered in your relationships with extroverts:

#1. Misunderstandings

It's not at all uncommon for extroverts to misunderstand their introverted friends and family members, and, of course, the flip side of that is also true.

For example, extroverts may think that you're upset with them, or that something else is wrong, simply because you're quiet.

#2. People who want you to socialize

Social expectations are probably one of the most common problems that crop up between introverts and extroverts. Your extroverted friends or family members may want to do a lot of social things, not understanding why you sometimes want to stay home.

For example, when a couple where one spouse is an introvert and the other is an extrovert goes to a big gathering—such as church—the extrovert may want to stay and chat until just about everyone else has left. In contrast, the introvert may run for the door as soon as the closing hymn ends.

#3. Your need for quiet

If you're an introvert who also thrives on silence, it may be difficult to be around talkative family members and friends.

For instance, an important part of Steve's day is his reading time—both for pleasure and for his business. On the other hand, his wife is social and enjoys conversations. At first, this created some conflict, but they eventually came to an agreement where they each get a little of what they want—conversation and reading time.

As you can see, it's easy to have conflict when extroverts and introverts are in a close relationship. Fortunately, we do have a few solutions that can alleviate—even prevent—some of the conflict that often arises.

Solutions to Challenge #13

If you have close relationships with extroverts, there are two strategies you can use to manage the problems that often occur:

#1. Have a dialogue about your differences.

When her children were little, Rebecca had a sneaky way of conveying her need for quiet. She simply played "The Quiet Game" to silence the chatter. But as they got older, she explained her needs to them, and because of that, no one was offended when Rebecca pulled back.

You don't necessarily have to play games with others to communicate your needs, but we do suggest that you communicate some (or all) of the following with the important people in your life:

- Introverts need space. It has nothing to do with not wanting to be around the people you care about.
- Introverts also need alone time. Again, this has nothing to do with other people; it is just the way you are.
- Introverts don't let many people in. If they share things with you, it really means something.
- Don't try to *fix* an introvert. We aren't broken.
- When an introvert does talk, don't interrupt. Interrupting introverts is a sure way for them to shut down. On the

other hand, as an introvert, you also have to leave room for others to speak.

- Introverts hate confrontation. Give them a little time to think things through rather than trying to press for an immediate resolution.

- When an introvert loves someone, they are very loyal and expect the same in return.

We'll admit that a good portion of this communication process can come across as selfish, so that's why it's important to make concessions for others. Sometimes this means doing certain things that you might not enjoy—like going to a social event.

With that in mind, you should also...

#2. Balance your "downtime" with strengthening your relationship(s).

For relationships to work, there should be balance—a give and take between both people in the relationship. This means sometimes you have the flexibility to retreat into your cave. Other times, it means you engage in outgoing, extrovert activities that might not seem enjoyable.

By working together (and with some mutual understanding), extroverts and introverts can have fantastic relationships.

In Challenge #2, we shared some great insights from John E. We really like one specific comment that we'll share again:

"I am also married. My wife did not understand why I did not want to go out on a Friday night. The amount of energy I would have to expend throughout the weekday being gregarious and social is exhausting. I need to recharge at nights and retreat inwards for two hours. So we made a compromise that we would plan weekend activities in advance and not go out on Friday nights."

What John shared is a great example of a healthy compromise in a relationship between an introvert and an extrovert.

While John didn't explicitly state that they talked this through, it's obvious they did. Otherwise, they wouldn't have come to this compromise. The solution they came up with has a nice, healthy balance and, because of that, both of their needs have been met.

Challenge #14: Networking

Does the word "networking" make you cringe? If so, welcome to the club!

Networking is one of the most common complaints about being an introvert. In fact, many introverts have openly expressed the desire to be more outgoing and have the ability to network like an extrovert.

Perhaps you can relate to these words written by Bob, who responded to our poll. *"I'm told in books, articles, blogs, and websites that I just need to get out and do more networking, make speeches, and lead other people in order to make the "minor adjustments" that can become strengths for introverts. I take these things to mean I should just change and simply become an extrovert. No way!"*

We certainly understand how Bob feels. As we've previously mentioned, you can't change from introvert to extrovert, so when Bob says, "No way!" we agree that it's impossible to change your core personality.

Having said that, everyone (including introverts) can benefit from networking. The good news is that your networking doesn't have to be loud and flashy for it to work. All you really need to do is focus on building quality relationships instead of trying to be a social butterfly at every social gathering.

Small Talk (a Reminder)

As we previously mentioned, an aspect of networking that most introverts hate is small talk.

In fact, Barbara wrote, *"The biggest struggle for me is to network. I know, because I've seen it, that to be successful and well-known, you need to be...well-known. You need to network and it's difficult when, for some people, it's easier not to initiate conversations and be an observer. Not that we are rude and don't want to meet people, but sometimes it seems better to have a few good deep conversations than to have small talk with a lot of people."*

We've already covered many aspects of networking in previous chapters, specifically the section on small talk, so be sure to refer to that for a refresher. One comment we would like to touch on again is that you can reap the benefits of networking by focusing on a small number of people instead of large groups. Fortunately, this is an area where many introverts excel.

It Only Takes a Few People

One of the significant problems introverts have when it comes to networking is a feeling of *overwhelm*, due to the sheer number of people involved. This is especially true at conferences and other large networking events.

The good news is that you don't have to connect with a lot of people for networking to work. In fact, focusing on developing real relationships with a smaller number of people is a good approach, and it just happens to fit with how introverts are wired.

In the chapter "What is an Introvert?" Rebecca told the story of how she and Steve met, and how you don't have to be the life of the party to benefit from networking events. You can, instead, benefit from associating with extroverts who are at the event.

One of the best ways to do this is to "attach" yourself to an extrovert.

When Rebecca recently attended a conference, she felt a bit lost when she first walked in. She wasn't thrilled with the idea of jumping into conversations that were already happening. Thankfully, an extrovert reached out and "saved" her. She did so by introducing herself to Rebecca, and then they hung out for a good part of the evening. Rebecca found it easier to mix with other people with her new friend by her side.

Intentionality Helps

It helps to be intentional about what you want to accomplish as a result of attending an event. For example, when Rebecca saw Steve's name on a list of attendees for the business breakthrough event she was going to attend, she knew that he was someone she wanted to meet.

At the time, she had no thought of co-writing books with him but had read some of his published titles. Since she was interested in Kindle publishing, she knew he would be an interesting person to meet.

Rather than worrying about meeting a bunch of different people, she had the goal of meeting only one person. This reduced overwhelm because her objective was a small one. She didn't need to be the life of the party, and she didn't need to chat it up with everyone in the room. If she talked to just one person, she would have met her goal.

As you can see, networking doesn't have be that intimidating—especially when you create a goal to only meet and make a connection with a small number of people.

To help you do this, we've included a few suggestions below to help you make the most out of every networking opportunity.

Solutions to Challenge #14

Many of the strategies necessary to network effectively were covered in previous sections (like Challenge #5 and Challenge #6), so we won't waste your time by repeating them here. What we do recommend (if you struggle with networking) is to review these sections before your next social interaction.

That said, we do have a few additional strategies to help you make the most of the connections you hope to make.

Strategy 1: Determine what you need from networking.

As mentioned above, it helps to be intentional when attending a networking event. You can carry this intentionality further by having an overall objective for networking. The reason why may change over time, but you should always understand what you would like to get out of each social encounter and, more importantly, what value you can provide to others.

For example, you may use networking to find a job at one point in your life and make business contacts at another point. If you have a special skillset at your job, you can be a good contact for others who struggle in this area. Remember: The best networking happens when each person provides value to the other.

Strategy 2: Practice small talk.

Review the section on small talk (Challenge #6), and implement these strategies everywhere you go. Trust us, knowing how to engage in small talk will make networking easier.

Strategy 3: Develop relationships online.

Social media, forums, blogs, and online mastermind groups have helped open many doors for introverts who hate to network in person. For many of us, it's easier to initiate conversations when you're able to hide behind a computer monitor (although we do stress the importance of balancing this activity with in-person events).

Strategy 4: Attend small events.

Look for events that are small, and attend them when possible. For example, many Meetup groups only have a handful of people attending each event. When you go to one of these events, it's harder to hide, which forces you to get involved in conversations.

We recommend that you attend at least two live events per month. This frequency might seem scary, but you'll quickly discover that it's easy to build up your networking skills when you regularly meet new people and engage them in conversation.

Strategy 5: Set a small goal for each networking event.

Remember that Rebecca had one goal when attending the business breakthrough event—meet Steve. That said, she ended up talking to just about everyone at the event. The point here is Rebecca would have already considered the event a success, since she accomplished her one goal, but she gained "bonus points" by talking to lots of other business owners.

Another thing to realize is you might not know anyone at the event. If that's the case, your small goal is to meet and have a significant conversation with *at least* one person. If you have a chance to meet lots of people, then your time at the event was *really* successful.

Strategy 6: Act fast.

In response to our poll, Pascal wrote, "*At a conference or a party I force myself to 'plunge in' and stand in the middle of the room and as soon as I enter start introducing myself to people. If I hesitate I'm lost and might as well go home there and then.*"

We'll be the first to admit that this seems challenging, but we recommend this advice because it recognizes that many introverts hesitate to call attention to themselves.

So, the next time you walk into a networking event, make it a point to talk to the first person you see. In a way, opening your mouth and immediately starting a conversation is like quickly ripping off a Band-Aid. You know you have to do it, so you might as well get it over with as soon as possible.

Strategy 7: Follow up.

Many people waste networking connections due to poor follow-up. For example, you might receive several business cards and hand out several of your own, but this means nothing if you're not connecting with people afterward.

We suggest that you choose at least one person to follow up with after an event. The great thing is, you can follow up in comfortable ways, such as email or social media. What's important is to make a commitment to follow up and then *actually* do it.

Challenge #15: Not Being Seen as a Leader

Many introverts feel that, due to their personalities, they're not seen as people who demonstrate strong leadership. This is exacerbated by the fact that many people view leaders as people who are extremely outgoing and personable, traits that aren't natural to many introverts.

But introverts can be great leaders. They just need to highlight their natural strengths.

Consider some of these strengths that most introverts have:

They think first and talk later. Because of this, an introvert is much less likely to put a foot in his mouth. This is a great attribute for leaders, especially since people really listen to what leaders say. Many extroverted leaders have said things they've regretted. While introverts sometimes say the wrong thing, it's less likely to happen due to their tendency to think before speaking.

They remain calm. Leaders have to deal with crises on a regular basis. Being calm in the midst of a crisis is an essential leadership trait.

They learn and understand the depth of issues. Introverts see beneath the surface and pick up on things that many extroverts miss. That type of insight is vital for big decisions that leaders make.

Introverts are excellent listeners. They are more apt to hear everyone out and weigh the words others say before jumping to conclusions.

They are excellent at preparation. Introverts typically show up at meetings with all of their ducks in a row, and because of it, time is spent more wisely and efficiently.

Introverts are great strategists. Strategy is a vital skill for leaders. Since introverts think deeply and listen closely, they are better equipped to come up with solid strategies.

Introverts notice "quiet influencers" (other introverts) and know how to get the most out of them.

Introverts are good at identifying what needs to change.

By highlighting their strengths rather than worrying about their weaknesses, introverts can be great leaders. In fact, we feel that the introspective qualities of introverts give them the potential to be the very best leaders.

To learn more about leadership, we recommended two books by Jim Collins: *Built to Last* and *Good to Great*. In these books, Collins shares findings that indicate that the CEOs of the most effective companies are introverts.

This shouldn't be too surprising; just think of the following introverts and how much they've impacted the world:

- Gandhi
- Mitt Romney
- Barack Obama
- Warren Buffet
- Bill Gates
- Abraham Lincoln
- Eleanor Roosevelt

The bottom line is that introverts can be everything from CEOs to presidents, so never let being an introvert hold you back from pursuing leadership positions!

Solutions to Challenge #15

Don't think you have what it takes to an effective leader? If so, here are a few strategies we recommend to unlock your ability to take charge of a group.

Step 1: Change your mindset.

To be a leader, and to be recognized by others as one, you first need to accept the fact that you have what it takes to be a leader. So if you've believed the lie that introverts can't be leaders, stop it!

Step 2: Change your perception of a leader.

Leaders don't all have to be loud and outgoing. Some people lead in very quiet ways. Rosa Parks is a great example. While Martin Luther King was the mouthpiece of the civil rights movement, Rosa is also frequently mentioned. *What did she do?* She impacted the world by sitting quietly. No loud speeches or demonstrations necessary. She just stuck to her convictions, in her own quiet way.

Step 3: Ring your own bell.

You don't have to be obnoxious about it, but don't downplay your accomplishments. Refer back to Challenge #12 for tips for dealing with your accomplishments not being recognized.

Step 4: Build your public speaking skills.

We've talked a lot about the fact that you can't change from being an introvert to an extrovert, but you can develop skills that many leaders need. One of those is public speaking.

Start small by taking a public speaking class or joining an organization such as Toastmasters. While it's true that, like Rosa Parks, you can have a big impact without being loud, you may be asked to do some public speaking when you are a leader. Start preparing now.

Step 5: Use content to demonstrate your expertise.

Blogging and other types of media are a great way to demonstrate your knowledge and insight. You can create the content in the privacy of your home or office and post it online. This is a great way to show that you really know your stuff. In fact, through blogging, video creation, podcasting, and other types of content, you can become known as a thought leader in your industry.

Steve feels he's a good example of this. While he doesn't give public speeches, he's often regarded as an expert (or leader) on self-publishing. How did he do this? Simply by creating online content that details the accomplishments of his book-based business.

Hopefully these examples demonstrate that you don't have to be loud or super-social to be recognized as a leader. All you have to do is recognize the value you provide to the world and be transparent about how you can help others. You'll find that people will naturally gravitate toward you.

Three Things to Do Today...

We've reached the end of the book.

Hopefully you've gained a new perspective on what it means to be an introvert. Perhaps you've picked up a strategy or two on how to overcome specific personal challenges, or maybe you've gained the confidence you need to take a stand against a person causing problems in your life. No matter what, we hope this book has helped you in some small way.

Now, as we close things out, we recommend three things to help you turn this information into action.

#1. Focus on Your Top Challenge

We covered 15 different challenges faced by introverts. Honestly, it would be impossible to tackle all of them at once. Your mind (and busy schedule) doesn't have the capacity to add dozens of new habits into your life. In fact, we urge you to focus on one challenge, identify the best way to overcome it and create a daily habit that reinforces this behavior.

For instance, let's say you often struggle in a social setting. This can include a variety of challenges like making a good first impression (Challenge #5), engaging in small talk (Challenge #6) and networking (Challenge #14). All of these issues would be impossible to overcome in the next few weeks, so a simpler solution is to start with a single activity.

So let's say you realize that most of your issues stem from not knowing *what to say* whenever you're in a conversation. What we would suggest is to create a daily habit where you engage one person in a conversation. That's it. Just one new person every day to practice your skills at small talk.

Once you've become comfortable with this habit, try two a day, then three a day. Keep repeating this until you're perfectly comfortable with the idea of talking to people in a variety of conversations.

#2. Review Your Specific Solutions

As we mentioned at the top of the book, not all of the challenges will apply to you. Remember there are eight types of introverts. That means you probably excel where others don't, while you have limitations in areas that some folks have mastered. The point here is the best use of your time is to identify the specific challenges you regularly encounter.

Our suggestion is simple. Once you've identified the areas where you struggle, go back to the relevant challenge and review the solutions we gave you for overcoming your specific issues. Some of these suggestions might require you to form a daily habit, while others might simply require a daily action. The point here is to understand what needs to be done and make a plan for it.

#3. Schedule Time

Information is nothing without action. If your goal is to overcome some of the challenges you face as an introvert, then you need to set aside time each day to work on this area of your life.

The simplest way to do this is to anchor the habit you want to form to a routine you consistently do every single day.

As an example, if you always start your computer in the morning, then you can add a new habit to this established routine. Reinforce the new habit by creating a statement like this: *"When I start my computer in the morning, I will send one outreach email to a person in my industry."*

As you see, it doesn't take much to build new habits into your life. In fact, we highly recommend that you start small and focus on consistency instead of setting a goal that's too big to achieve.

Well, we've reached the end of the *conversation* about introversion. Now the ball is in your court. All that we ask is for you to think of the one area of your life where you struggle the most and make a commitment to do something about it on a daily basis.

We believe in you, but for you to succeed at overcoming these challenges, you need to believe in yourself. After reading this book, you have all of the information you need to identify your biggest challenges and use your introspective qualities to succeed at work and in life.

We wish you the best of luck!

Steve "S.J." Scott
www.DevelopGoodHabits.com

Rebecca Livermore
www.ProfessionalContentCreation.com

Did You Like *Confident You?*

Before you go, we'd like to say "thank you" for purchasing our book.

You could have picked from dozens of books on habit development, but you took a chance and checked out this one.

So a big thanks for downloading this book and reading all the way to the end.

Now we'd like ask for a *small* favor. **Could you please take a minute or two and leave a review for this book on Amazon?**

This feedback will help us continue to write the kind of Kindle books that help you get results. And if you loved it, then please let us know. :-)

More Books by Rebecca

- *Level Up Your Day: How to Maximize the 6 Essential Areas of Your Daily Routine*

- *The Daily Entrepreneur: 33 Success Habits for Small Business Owners, Freelancers and Aspiring 9-to-5 Escape Artists*

- *Blogger's Quick Guide to Writing Rituals and Routines*

- *Content Repurposing Made Easy: How to Create More Content in Less Time to Expand Your Reach*

More Books by Steve

- *10-Minute Declutter: The Stress-Free Habit for Simplifying Your Home*
- *Exercise Enough: 32 Tactics for Building the Exercise Habit (Even If You Hate Working Out)*
- *The Daily Entrepreneur: 33 Success Habits for Small Business Owners, Freelancers and Aspiring 9-to-5 Escape Artists*
- *Level Up Your Day: How to Maximize the 6 Essential Areas of Your Daily Routine*
- *Master Evernote: The Unofficial Guide to Organizing Your Life with Evernote (Plus 75 Ideas for Getting Started)*
- *Bad Habits No More: 25 Steps to Break ANY Bad Habit*
- *Habit Stacking: 97 Small Life Changes That Take Five Minutes or Less*
- *To-Do List Makeover: A Simple Guide to Getting the Important Things Done*
- *23 Anti-Procrastination Habits: How to Stop Being Lazy and Get Results in Your Life*
- *S.M.A.R.T. Goals Made Simple: 10 Steps to Master Your Personal and Career Goals*

- *115 Productivity Apps to Maximize Your Time: Apps for iPhone, iPad, Android, Kindle Fire and PC/iOS Desktop Computers*

- *Writing Habit Mastery: How to Write 2,000 Words a Day and Forever Cure Writer's Block*

- *Declutter Your Inbox: 9 Proven Steps to Eliminate Email Overload*

- *Wake Up Successful: How to Increase Your Energy and Achieve Any Goal with a Morning Routine*

- *10,000 Steps Blueprint: The Daily Walking Habit for Healthy Weight Loss and Lifelong Fitness*

- *70 Healthy Habits: How to Eat Better, Feel Great, Get More Energy and Live a Healthy Lifestyle*

- *Resolutions That Stick! How 12 Habits Can Transform Your New Year*

All books can be found at: www.developgoodhabits.com